Love Up Your List
Grow Your Tribe
(and Increase Sales)
with Email Marketing

JEN LEVITZ
SpellbindingBusinessSchool.com

CONTENTS

INTRODUCTION

Hello and welcome to this book on email marketing.

So you've setup a list, added a few emails into your autoresponder, sent people to a squeeze page, given them a gift in exchange for their email… then you sit there and wonder why people don't open up your emails.

Here's a question for you:

Why should anybody ever read your emails? Why should they read your email, instead of everybody else's email?

Let's take a look at this scenario; if you're like me, you probably get 100+ emails per day from people whose lists you're on, that doesn't even include the 200 emails from spammers.

So of those 100 emails per day, how many do you think I open? Maybe 5, maybe 6. So that's about a 5-6% open rate from my own personal account.

Now why do I open only a handful of emails each day?

The truth is I only open emails from a certain number of people, and I literally open their emails every single time they send me one. These people (there are probably about 5-10 of them) are marketers that I respect highly, and whom I think I can learn something from.

Did you get that?

I respect them. They know a lot more than I do in certain areas. They make more money than I do. I trust them. I like them. I can learn from them.

I imagine you do the same thing with a certain number of marketers who send you emails, and I'm guessing pretty much everybody else does the same thing as well.

So what does this mean for you and your business?

If you're actively building your list and you want to get your emails opened more often, you have to become one of these marketers that people respect, and actually want to hear from.

That means you have to provide your subscribers with more information than the next guy, you have to provide them with better information, you have to be more trustworthy, more respected, more well liked…basically you have to become one of your subscribers' 'must open' marketers.

You have to become one of those people who provides subscribers with so much value that they actually look forward to your emails, and will not just open your emails, but will actively read it and click through on the links you include.

So how do you get there? How do you become a 'must open' marketer?

You over deliver.

You give out only the best information and advice, make it more interesting, more valuable, and more useful than anything the next guy is going to write.

And this is exactly what we're going to cover in this book.

So let's get right into it...

Jen Levitz

SpellbindingBusinessSchool.com

P.S. As you are going through this book, if something comes up for you and you have a question or concern, do us both a favor and reach out to me. I really do want to help you make more money and serve more people in your business.

JEN LEVITZ

CHAPTER 1

WHAT'S THE PURPOSE OF YOUR EMAIL CAMPAIGN?

Before you write a single email, or make a single dollar from your list, the first thing you absolutely have to do is to determine what it is you actually want to accomplish with your email campaign.

What is the purpose of your campaign?

Most people that are just starting out will think they have to start building a list purely because everybody is telling them that "the money is in the list".

But having a list in and of itself is useless. The list by itself does not make you sales and profits – it's what you do with that list that creates sales and profits.

You need to have a purpose for why you are building your list and creating an email campaign.

Perhaps you're working for a non-profit organization and you want to spread the word about your cause. Or maybe you've just written a new course, or created a new product, and you want to drum up sales.

Whatever your purpose is, you need to make sure that every email you write in your campaign draws you closer to achieving that goal.

If your email doesn't move subscribers closer to taking the action you want them to, then it will gradually detract them away from your purpose.

So if you want to sell your new course or your $97 product, everything you do as part of your list building and email campaign should build up to people making a purchase from you.

Now, that doesn't mean that every email you send them is a promo for your product, instead it's actually the complete opposite; every email should be building more rapport with your subscribers so that they come to know, like, and trust you enough to purchase your course, your training, your video product, or whatever it is you're trying to sell to them.

Each of your emails should be building credibility, it should be building trust, and it should be making your subscribers more comfortable with the idea of buying your product.

So you need to know what your purpose is when creating your email campaign, and that also determines the next chapter.

CHAPTER 2

HOW TO ORGANIZE YOUR EMAIL CAMPAIGN

To move people closer to making a purchase from you, you don't just send them sales emails all day. You need to use a number of different types of emails in your email campaign.

You need to write content emails, referral emails, free gift emails, and feedback emails. All of these emails should bring people closer to your goal for your list.

So what you should do is send your list a lot of very useful content early on. You should have already provided them with a free gift for subscribing to your list, now in the first few emails you should send them more useful information that builds on what you covered in your free gift.

The more value you provide early, the more receptive your subscribers will be to your promotional emails later on.

What you're doing with these initial emails is you are building long term reciprocity. So if you give something of value to someone, they will not only feel grateful but they will feel as though they want to give something back to you.

In your case, the more valuable information you provide to your subscribers, the more likely they are to feel comfortable purchasing your products later on.

A lot of people balk at the thought of giving away valuable information and knowledge for free. They want their subscribers to pay for their best information, but here's the problem with this type of thinking; how would your subscribers know that you are knowledgeable if you don't give them valuable and high quality information for free to begin with?

If you think you don't have enough knowledge or advice to actually give away for free, then you need to learn more. Study more about your niche, read, buy training products for your own knowledge.

So your campaign should be organized based on the premise that you need to give first by providing high quality, valuable information to build credibility, and then you will receive later when your subscribers buy your products.

CHAPTER 3

HOW TO CREATE CREDIBILITY WITH YOUR TRIBE

Having credibility with your subscribers is absolutely critical to your success. If your subscribers don't trust you or don't believe you know what you're talking about, then they sure as heck aren't going to buy from you.

If you want them to buy anything from you, then you have to make them trust you first.

So how do you do that?

There are two important ways to achieve trust and build credibility with your subscribers.

One important way is to be congruent in everything you do and say. You can't say one thing in one email, then a few days later say something that contradicts that in another email. You also can't tell your list to do things a certain way, then you go and do something completely different. You need to be consistent and congruent in everything you say and do.

People will spot the inconsistencies right away and it hurts your credibility and your trust levels significantly.

The other important way you can build credibility with your subscribers is to over deliver.

Now that doesn't just mean providing more information, or more content, it also means providing better information and better content.

It means giving people more value than they expect.

What some successful marketers do is on their download pages, in addition to the product people bought from them, there are a few additional free gifts they give to people. These are unadvertised bonuses that provides more value than is expected. They don't have to do it, but they do.

They over deliver.

Do you think you could do something like that as well? Just provide a few extra bonuses that are related to what people just bought or are looking to download.

What you could also do when you tell people you will give them a free gift for opting into your list is to also give them 2 or 3 extra free gifts in the first email alone. Then you could go another extra mile and give them a few more over the next few days.

So you promised to give them one free gift if they opt-in to your list, they got that, but they also got several additional free gifts without needing to take any further action.

The key here is to make those other free gifts just as, or even more, valuable than the one they signed up to download.

That's how you over deliver, and that's how you build trust and create credibility with your subscribers.

When you do that, your subscribers are going to look forward to your emails, and they're going to open up their wallets for you.

CHAPTER 4

HOW TO CREATE RAPPORT WITH YOUR TRIBE

Along with building trust and credibility with your subscribers, another critical thing you have to do is build rapport with them.

You have to get the people on your list to believe that you care about them, and that you are there to support them and help them, not just to make sales off of them.

Now, most of them will realize that you are making money by selling products to them, but they have to believe your intentions are primarily to help them first, rather than just using them to make sales.

You have to exchange something of value for the money they give you when they buy your products.

Just like if you go to a day job, your company will pay you, but first you have to give them something that is worth what they will pay you. You need to first do your job, whatever it might be, in order to get paid.

You are exchanging something of value (your time, knowledge, skill etc.) for something else of value (in the case of a job, it's a salary).

And it's the same thing with your email list.

They aren't going to just buy something from you because you want them to; you need to first exchange your knowledge or talent with them, before they buy anything from you.

You have to help your subscribers first, then they will pay you, and you accomplish this by creating rapport with your subscribers.

How do you do this?

There are two things you need to do here:

1. You have to give valuable information and advice to them first
2. You have to interact with them on a personal level

So with the first one, it's a pretty common feeling among us humans that if you give something to someone, they feel obligated to give something back in return.

The same principle applies online with your email list. You need to give your subscribers something of value first, and in return some will reciprocate by buying something from you.

The more you give – whether that is free eBooks within your niche, videos or audios teaching them something specific, or just specific tips and tactics you've discovered – the more likely people on your list will feel the need to give back to you, and usually they do that by buying your products.

So one part of building rapport with your subscribers is to give first; the second is to interact with them on a personal level.

Now you do this by actually communicating with your subscribers individually.

One way to achieve this is to send your subscribers feedback emails. We'll cover how to write feedback emails a bit later in this book, but basically what you do with feedback emails is you send your subscribers an email asking them for feedback about something specific.

You ask them something about what problems they're facing in your niche, and you tell them that you will reply to their questions personally.

So if you're in the weight loss niche, and you ask your subscribers to send you questions they have about ab workouts, you're going to get a bunch of replies with questions like what's the most effective workout, or how often they should workout?

The key is you need to respond to the emails you get from your subscribers personally. I know this will take a few minutes each, but you're generally going to get very similar questions.

What you're doing here is setting yourself apart from the rest of the marketers out there who just automate their email marketing.

When you actually interact with your subscribers on a personal level, they will see you more as a friend and a trusted adviser than just a faceless marketer on the Internet.

They're going to come to know, like, and trust you – you're building rapport – and this is the difference between being a successful email marketer, and just a regular email marketer who doesn't make any sales.

The more rapport you can build with your subscribers – by giving them high value information first, and interacting with them personally – the greater your chances are of making sales over the long term from your list.

Most people don't take the time to build this rapport with their list, which is why they struggle to make any sales.

Don't do what they do.

Take the time to build rapport with your list and they will reward you for that.

CHAPTER 5

HOW YOU SHOULD WRITE YOUR EMAILS

So now you know why you're creating a list, and what your purpose for your email campaign is, it's time to actually get started putting things together.

And it all starts with writing emails.

Now most people when they see this will think there is some magic formula for writing emails that gets people to open every time, get people to click on every link, and hypnotize them into buying products from them over and over again.

Unfortunately, this isn't the case. There is no magical formula, there is no secret tactic, and there is no blueprint to success with email marketing.

You see, if there really was a formula and everybody in-the-know was using it, then you would get bored very fast.

Your emails would be just like mine and everyone else's emails that followed the same formula.

Think about it; if you were exchanging emails with someone, it could be a good friend, an acquaintance, a family member, anybody, and every email you got from this person was written exactly the same way every time, like it was based on a formula. For example, they always opened with the same few lines, and always told a quick story about what happened to them that day, and then they always asked you for some advice with a problem they're having. Obviously it can be any formula, but the point is it is the same type of email based on the exact same formula every single time.

What would happen if you received the same type of email every day from this person?

You know what would happen; you would get very bored of their emails, very quickly.

Now what would happen if that person emailed you often but in a sporadic nature, where sometimes they would tell a great story, other times they ask you for advice, and even every now and then they recommend a great new website or tool they found yesterday.

Maybe some of the emails will just ramble on, whereas others get right down to the point. The difference is you don't know what to expect. You don't know what's going to be in the next email, whether they will be happy or sad, or if they're going to be angry or peaceful. But the point here is there will be anticipation and excitement in waiting for their next email.

That is exactly how your emails should be as well. You want your subscribers to eagerly anticipate your next email and be excited to receive it.

If you make them predictable, boring or unexciting, your subscribers won't be looking forward to reading your emails at all. That's how most marketers write their emails.

But if your emails are fresh and different, you write from the heart and with genuine honesty, you're going to be seen differently by your subscribers.

Write with your own personal style and personality; don't try to be someone else.

The main thing is you need to stay away from the idea that you need a formula or a template to write successful emails.

People who use these so-called blueprints are those who don't get any results. They don't put their own personality into their emails, they don't write from the heart, and they don't really care about their subscribers; they just hope they can put together a few email swipes from an affiliate product and make some sales.

Don't do this.

You need to write from your heart. You need to write to your subscribers like you're writing to a good friend. You should envision that you are writing to just one person when you are writing your emails – just one person – then send that to your entire list.

Yes, some people aren't going to like your emails or your style, that's fine; just let them opt out of your list. If they don't like your emails, there's a good chance they're not going to buy from you, so who cares if they leave?

If you write enough emails from your heart, you're going to keep the subscribers who view you as someone they know, like, and trust. And these subscribers are the ones who are going to buy from you over and over again.

So write your emails from your heart. Show that you actually care about your subscribers and that you want the best from them.

CHAPTER 6

WRITING HEADLINES FOR YOUR EMAILS

The headline is one of the most important parts of your email. The headline is what draws the reader's attention to your email. It tells them what the email is about and allows them to determine if they're going to open it up or not.

The headline is often what dictates if only a few people open your emails or whether a large portion of your list opens your email.

Of course the best way to get people to actually open and read your emails is to develop a relationship with your subscribers, but a good headline is still important in convincing your subscribers that your email is worth reading.

So here are some headline ideas you can use in your own campaigns:

Benefit Headlines: These headlines let your subscribers know that they will be getting a specific benefit once they open and read the email. A few examples could be:

Lose 10 pounds in 7 days…?

How you can train your puppy to stay

Discover the secrets of selling your own books online…

Problem Headlines: These headlines highlight a problem the subscribers might be going through and presume to offer a solution within the email. For example:

Are you struggling to lose your belly fat? Not anymore!

Need relief from stress? Check this out…

Embarrassed by your hair loss? You need to see this!

How-To Headlines: These headlines tell the subscribers they are going to learn 'how to' do something within the email. Here are a few examples:

How to lose 10 pounds in the next 21 days!

How to potty train your child in 3 days!

How to win friends and influence people

Direct Command Headlines: These headlines tell the subscribers to do something specific, for example:

Read this if you want to discover the secret of growing pumpkins!

Get started with your own online business today!

Stop struggling to lose weight today!

Question Headlines: These headlines ask subscribers a question about some problem they are going through. Here are a few examples:

How long have you struggled to lose your belly fat?

Do you need help with your marriage?

Why haven't you started making a full time income online?

Offer Headlines: These headlines present a specific offer to the subscriber, for example:

Free shipping on all books ordered today!

20% off if you order today!

Buy one get one free…24 hours only!

Use these headline examples in your own email campaigns. Obviously use your own offers and benefits to fit your subscribers.

CHAPTER 7

WRITING A CALL-TO-ACTION IN YOUR EMAIL

One of the most important parts of your actual email is your call-to-action. You don't write emails to your list just for the sake of writing emails.

You also want them to take some kind of action.

You want them to click on a link to read a blog post, or to watch a video, or to check out a new product you just released.

Basically, you want them to take a specific action, and to do this, you have to tell them specifically what they need to do.

So when you write a call-to-action in your email, don't be afraid to be direct. Tell people exactly what to do. You don't want any of your subscribers to read your email and then wonder what they are supposed to do after reading the email.

Here are a few examples of some good calls-to-action:

Click here to get started.

Check out this video to get the full details.

If you want to learn more, just go here:

Of course you want to either make that call-to-action a link to the page you want to send your subscribers, or just have the actual URL next to or below the call-to-action.

CHAPTER 8

HOW TO WRITE CONTENT EMAILS

Content emails should really be the backbone of your email campaign. This is where you provide high value advice and information to your subscribers, and it's also how you build a relationship with them. The more great content you provide to them, the more they will come to know, like, and trust you.

So how do you write content emails?

Basically you write them like you would write articles.

If you have something you want to share with your readers – it might be a useful tip, some advice, a solution to a problem – then just write a short article about it.

The only difference between writing an article and a content email is that with the email you just use shorter sentences and shorter paragraphs to improve readability.

The key with content emails is to also write them like you are standing in front of them and discussing this issue with them. You make it more personal that way.

What you can do to open the email is tell the readers why you want to share this piece of content with them. So it could be because you get a lot of questions about it, or because it's something you've been thinking about lately, or because it's something new. Tell them why you are writing this piece of content for them.

Then get right to the point and tell them the tip or piece of advice you want to share with them.

You also want to make the content email action oriented. So for example, you might write a content email about how to do something better. Once you've shared the information with them, then give them a set of action steps they can instantly apply. It doesn't have to be extensive, just a couple of steps should do. You want them to take action when they finish reading your email.

This does two things; first it makes your email stand out. Most times with content emails people will just skim through them and take in the main points. But when you have action steps in your email, it makes the reader stop and actually think about what you're saying.

The second thing having action steps accomplishes is that it trains your readers to take action when they read your emails. You will also have other emails in your campaign where you want them to click through to your blog or sales page, so this gets them into the habit of clicking links in your emails. It builds trust. So when they see the links in your emails, they know they are going to be sent to a high quality page.

You want them to get comfortable clicking links in your emails so when it comes time for you to promote a product to them, they will be comfortable clicking the link to checkout the sales page.

CHAPTER 9

HOW TO WRITE FREE GIFT EMAILS

These are some of the easiest emails you'll write, but they're also some of the most effective when it comes to building a relationship with your subscribers.

Basically what you're doing is providing your subscribers with a free gift. Of course it's not just for the sake of it, it's so you can build reciprocity like we spoke about earlier in this book. The more high quality content you provide to your subscribers, the more they will feel like they need to reciprocate later on.

So with these emails what you want to do is keep it really simple.

Just create a short PDF report or audio or video. It can be anything that provides some high quality advice. It can just be one tip or one piece of advice, but make sure it can genuinely benefit your subscribers.

Then within the actual email, just keep it short and sweet; tell them you created a report, or video, for them, and that they can download it for free.

Don't try to sell anything to them in the email or within the free gift.

Just give them the gift, no strings attached. You will be rewarded for it later.

CHAPTER 10

HOW TO WRITE PROMOTIONAL EMAILS

These emails are the ones where you really make your money. Well, actually you really make your money when you build a strong relationship with your subscribers, but these promotional emails are where you collect the money.

The secret to writing successful promotional emails is that the better your relationship is with your list, the easier it will be to promote something to them.

If you have built a solid relationship with your subscribers by sending them free content and free gifts that are all high quality and valuable, then you have already created the trust necessary for them to be comfortable clicking through to your sales page and checking out the product you are offering.

If you're sending subscribers to your own product pages, then they will be used to reading your style and personality, but if you're sending them to an affiliate product then you need to tie them into your own credibility in your email.

You see if you're sending them to an affiliate offer created by someone they've never heard of before, you need to put their mind at ease and tell them that they can trust this person as well.

So what you can do to tie in the affiliate offer with your own credibility with your list is by talking about how you have benefited from this product.

Tell them about a problem you were having and how you struggled with this problem for a long time, before you found this product and used it for yourself. The product worked for you, so that's why you want to recommend that same product to your subscribers.

Basically what you're saying is that this product is good enough for you, so it's good enough to share with your subscribers as well.

Remember your subscribers trust you, so if you recommend something, there's a good chance they're going to check it out.

If you're promoting a product you've just created, then tell your subscribers that this is a new product and you want them to check it out.

Keep it short and simple.

Something else you can do if you are promoting a product that isn't new is to qualify the readers first. So you could write something like:

"Do you want to learn how to create high-converting squeeze pages?

Then check this out: "

So you qualify people to ensure that only people who want to learn about this specific lesson will click through, which is going to mean your sales page converts at a much higher rate.

CHAPTER 11

HOW TO WRITE FEEDBACK EMAILS

Feedback emails are when you send an email to your subscribers asking for feedback about something specific, and requesting that they actually reply to the email and give you their answers.

It's something most people won't ever do...but it's probably one of the most valuable emails you can send to your list.

A lot of marketers just want their email marketing to be completely automated – they just want to upload emails into their autoresponder and have them go out automatically – and they don't bother to interact with their subscribers much on a personal level.

But when you send feedback emails, you are doing a few important things all at the same time.

First you're finding out what your list wants to learn more about, and when you know that it's easy for you to provide it to them.

You also show them that you a real person who wants and values their feedback.

At the same time if you personally answer their email, that will set you apart from the rest of the marketers online who they don't have a personal connection with.

So you're building a closer relationship with your subscribers when you use feedback emails. It creates an incredible sense of personalization that most marketers don't ever bother with.

After you send your subscribers a feedback email, some of them will reply, what you should do is actually read through the emails.

Make note of some of the more common questions – generally most of the emails will have similar questions. Just list those common questions out in a text document like Notepad. Once you've compiled a list of the common questions, answer them within Notepad.

Then reply back to every email personally. The questions that are common you can just copy and paste your answer within the individual email, but also make sure you answer the rest of their questions as well.

Now if you're thinking that answering each of the emails personally is a waste of time, think again. What you're doing is building a deeper relationship with your subscribers – they are real people – and if they actually reply to your email it means they are the type of person who does what you tell them to do.

They are likely going to be the same people who download your free gifts, who open up and read all of your content emails, and they are also most likely the same people who will buy from you again and again.

So the more you develop the relationship with these people, the more likely they are going to respond to the rest of your emails – including the emails where you are promoting a product.

Remember, all of your emails should be trying to build trust or build credibility. These feedback emails are perfect for you to build trust with subscribers who perhaps didn't completely trust you before – not enough to buy from you anyway – and by you replying to and interacting with them personally, you finally were able to get them to trust you enough to buy from you.

The more trust and the more credibility you build with your list, the more likely they are going to end up buying from you.

So use feedback emails and don't be afraid to respond personally to those emails.

CHAPTER 12

HOW TO WRITE EMAILS THAT GENERATE A RESPONSE

The key to getting a good response from your subscribers when you send them emails is to write each email as if you are writing to one person, and not to an entire list of people.

When you write as if you're communicating to an entire list, there's no personal connection being made.

When you write an email with just one person in mind, you make it personal and you get a much better response.

Now how do you do this consistently so you can make a personal connection in all of your emails?

You have to focus on writing your emails as if you're writing to one person, not a group of subscribers. Imagine you are writing a personal email to a friend. Imagine if one of your friend's is on your list, they signed up because they are interested in what you have to offer, and they want to hear from you. When you sit down to write an email, just imagine yourself writing a personal email to that one friend.

Don't write to a group. Don't use words like 'my subscribers' or 'my list'. Instead use the word 'you' often, like you would if you were writing an email to a friend.

Your subscribers will know they aren't the only person on your list, but when you address them individually and personally, they make a connection with you on a deeper level, and the level of trust and credibility will increase again.

The deeper your connection can be with each of the individuals on your list, the better the response will be from your list as a whole.

CHAPTER 13

HOW TO PROPERLY FORMAT YOUR EMAILS

Something most people don't pay enough attention to is the formatting of your emails. This is critical to getting a higher response to your emails.

If your emails aren't formatted correctly, it's going to be difficult for your subscribers to read them, or they might end up just not reading it at all.

One critical factor to keep in mind with formatting is that most autoresponder service providers will limit each line of your email to 65 characters wide.

What this means is that if your email goes over 65 characters on a line, the autoresponder service will wrap the text to the next line, which can generally make the email look pretty messy.

So what you want to do is to limit each line of your email to less than 65 characters. Just hit 'enter' before the 65 character limit and keep it consistent throughout the entire email.

Another thing you want to do to make your emails more readable is to keep your paragraphs short, and break them up with empty lines to create more white space.

Take a look at these two sample emails:

Email 1	Email 2
Lorem ipsum dolor sit amet, consectetur adipiscing elit. Quisque ultrices lectus odio, sit amet malesuada arcu malesuada eget. Suspendisse potenti. Sed sit amet consectetur tortor, sit amet condimentum diam. Suspendisse sit amet posuere magna, eu sollicitudin urna. Maecenas sed ullamcorper libero. Curabitur aliquam consequat adipiscing. Donec at ante vehicula, vehicula tellus id, interdum nisl. Sed nulla eros, ultricies a facilisis dictum, vehicula in ipsum. Aliquam consequat auctor quam, at faucibus dolor vulputate et. In quam dolor, faucibus vel odio et, vestibulum tincidunt nisl. Interdum et malesuada fames ac ante ipsum primis in faucibus. Quisque ullamcorper suscipit hendrerit. Etiam ut nisl tempus, faucibus sem in, interdum dolor. Maecenas porttitor lacus eget justo vehicula bibendum sed vel odio. Vestibulum augue dolor, venenatis in interdum et, fermentum et felis. Phasellus in massa at risus volutpat fermentum.	Lorem ipsum dolor sit amet, consectetur adipiscing elit. Quisque ultrices lectus odio, sit amet malesuada arcu malesuada eget. Suspendisse potenti. Sed sit amet consectetur tortor, sit amet condimentum diam. Suspendisse sit amet posuere magna, eu sollicitudin urna. Maecenas sed ullamcorper libero. Curabitur aliquam consequat adipiscing. Donec at ante vehicula, vehicula tellus id, interdum nisl. Sed nulla eros, ultricies a facilisis dictum, vehicula in ipsum. Aliquam consequat auctor quam, at faucibus dolor vulputate et. In quam dolor, faucibus vel odio et, vestibulum tincidunt nisl. Interdum et malesuada fames ac ante ipsum primis in faucibus.

As you can see, the way the first email is formatted would make it extremely difficult and cumbersome to read.

You need to format your emails similar to the second sample so it's easy to read and will actually get a decent response.

Use a lot of white space in your email to break up the sentences and paragraphs, and don't be afraid to emphasize specific sentences, like a call to action, on a single line by itself.

It will help to make it stand out from the rest of the email, so you're making it easier for the reader to see the most important parts of the email and take action on it.

CHAPTER 14

WHY YOU MUST WRITE YOUR OWN EMAILS

When it comes to writing high-response emails, a lot of people get worried.

They don't know how to write an effective email campaign.

So the first thing they might do is hire someone to write the emails for them, or they get a set of templates and write something based on them.

The problem is that you're not writing from your heart if you hire someone or write from a template. You need to write your own emails if you really want to have a personal connection with the people on your list.

This is a really important concept that not a lot of people will ever consider properly.

When you build a list, you're not just collecting a bunch of emails; you're really trying to build a series of relationships with a bunch of individuals.

Each person that is on your list and actually reads your emails is just one person, and to establish a trusting relationship with that one person you have to have consistency in your communication.

Imagine you're trying to establish a friendship with someone in person, but instead of actually talking to them yourself, you hire someone else to talk to them for you, or to tell you what to say.

What's going to happen?

Even if you're the one actually talking to the person, you might be saying what someone else is telling you to say, and if you do that, you're not the one building a relationship with that person – they are really communicating with a different person, not you!

It's the same thing when you write emails to your list.

When you hire someone else to write your emails for you, you are not communicating directly with your subscribers, and they are not making a connection with you. The truth is they are actually communicating with someone else – the person who wrote the emails.

They can't develop a bond with you if your emails are different in style or personality, or if they aren't consistent.

It's always a far better idea to write your own emails yourself, even for affiliate promotions. Don't use the standard emails people provide you to promote their products. The way it's written isn't you – it's not your personality, and it's not your style. Even if they say it generated a great response, the fact is it was effective on someone else's list because they have a connection with their list. You need to establish your own connection with your own list and write your own emails to them.

Now you might be thinking that you don't know how to write effective emails to your list.

The most important thing to do is just write. Just start writing your emails. Make a plan of what you want to write in each email; what's the main purpose of that email? Then just write.

Remember just imagine if you're writing that email to a friend you're trying to help; write from the heart.

You'll find that the more emails you write, the better you're going to get. Over time you'll be able to see in your stats which emails got a better response, and start making changes to your emails to include more of the elements that made your emails successful.

You don't need to learn everything about how to write effective emails; if you have written just one email to a friend, any type of email, then you already know what you need to do to write an effective email campaign.

In most cases you're also going to make adjustments to your email campaigns as you learn more about how to write effectively. Start tracking the response rates and open rates. You're going to quickly learn what works with your list and what doesn't.

You need to learn by doing; what works for my list, may or may not necessarily work for your list. The only way to find out what's going to be effective for you with your subscribers is to email them and track your results.

After you get your results, you make the necessary adjustments to make your email campaign even better. That's how successful marketers really become successful; they try something, then track the results, and make adjustments to improve their campaigns.

That's what you should be doing as well.

CHAPTER 15

HOW OFTEN SHOULD YOU BE MAILING YOUR COMMUNITY?

This is the type of question that pops up all the time when it comes to email marketing.

The fact is there are many different marketers that use many different frequencies of mailing. What works for one marketer might not necessarily work for another.

The reason is because each list is unique. Each list is a market on its own. Each list responds to different things.

Your list will respond differently to my list, and it's also different to everybody else's list, so it's difficult to say a certain frequency of mailing works better than something else.

However, there is one thing that is always consistent throughout all lists; the more frequently you email your list, the more sales you will end up making, the more unsubscribes you will get, the lower your open rates will be, and the lower your click through rates will be.

On the other hand, the less frequently you email your list, the higher your conversion rates will be, the fewer unsubscribes you will get, the higher your open rates will be and the higher your click through rates will be.

Now you might be thinking it's generally a better idea to mail less frequently if open rates and response rates are higher, but at the end of the day you still need to make sales, and generally speaking the more you email your list, the more sales you're going to make.

That doesn't mean you always send them sales emails; emailing them frequently means you email them with a combination of content emails, free gift emails, feedback emails, and sales emails.

Some marketers mail their list every day, others 2-3 times per week, even more will mail their list even less than that.

The bottom line is you need to test different frequencies with your own list and see what works the best for you.

Those marketers who email every day are probably making more sales overall, but they're getting more unsubscribes. Now if you're getting 50-100+ subscribers per day, you can afford to lose 20 people, for example, through unsubscribes when you email them daily. But if you're only get about 10-20 subscribers per day, you probably can't afford to email your list daily and risk getting 10 unsubscribes per day.

It all depends on how much traffic you're driving on a daily basis, how many subscribers you're getting, and how effective your emails are.

Another thing to keep in mind is you don't have to just stick with the same frequency forever. If you're just starting out and your list is growing slowly, maybe you can start off by emailing 1-2 times per week. Then as you grow your list faster, then you can increase the frequency of emails.

If you've got a few products available, perhaps you can mail more frequently to get some sales coming in.

But you need to keep in mind that you will get unsubscribes regardless of how often you email your list; the question is, can you replace those subscribers consistently?

Email marketing isn't just about sending emails to your list, it's also about continuing to build your list on a daily basis. You don't just build a list of 5000 and stop. You keep building your list every single day, and you continue to test what works with your growing list.

CHAPTER 16

HOW TO TRACK THE SUCCESS OF YOUR CAMPAIGNS

So we've talked about how important it is to track the effectiveness of your emails, and see where you can improve your campaign.

If you want to be successful with email marketing, you need to be able to measure how effective your emails are, what is actually making your emails effective, and what is just not working for you.

One way to measure how effective your emails are is by seeing how many sales you actually produce, but this will only work in isolation with promotional emails. It obviously doesn't work with content emails where you're not necessarily promoting a product for your subscribers to buy.

With most autoresponder services, they will be able to provide you with accurate stats about your emails and campaign.

So the most common email marketing metrics you should pay attention to are:

Delivery Rate
The email delivery rate refers to the percentage of emails that were actually delivered to your subscribers. This is an important indicator of the quality of the email leads you have in your list. If the delivery

rate is low, and you have focused on driving traffic from a particular source, then it indicates that the quality of that traffic source is suspect. You want the delivery rate to be as high as possible. The higher the delivery rate, the higher the quality of the leads on your list.

Open Rate

The open rate is the percentage of subscribers that actually opened the email you sent to them. This is one of the most important metrics you need to measure in your campaign.

If you have several emails in your campaign, and a few of them have higher open rates than average, take a closer look and see why that might be. Maybe it was a good headline. Maybe it was the benefits you mentioned. Whatever it was, pay close attention and implement that lesson into the rest of your campaign.

On the other hand, if some of your emails have much lower open rates than normal, it might indicate that their headlines are not effective and it might be worth changing them to test what else might work more effectively.

If your email open rate drops dramatically and stays at a lower rate than normal after a specific email, it might mean something in that email turned subscribers off your subsequent emails. If you see this happening, you need to take a closer look at the email immediately before the open rate drop occurred – what is within that email that might have turned your subscribers off? Did you promise something and didn't deliver? Did you promote a product that has a bad reputation? Was something wrong with the content or free gift you provided? Take a closer look, send a test email to yourself, click through to all the links, and read through the email again – you need to find out what the issue is and fix it.

Your subject line is the first thing people will see in their email inbox, and that is usually one of the biggest factors that will determine whether they open your email or not. So you need to work on improving your subject lines. The other important factor is you and the relationship you have with your subscribers. Like we mentioned earlier in the book, if you have a good relationship with your list, they are going to look forward to receiving your emails and open them once you send them.

Click Through Rate

The click through rate is the percentage of subscribers that actually clicks on one of the links in your email.

Aside from open rates, click through rates are probably the second biggest indicator of how effective your emails are.

A low click through rate might tell you that your subscribers don't trust you enough to click the links in your email, or that the content isn't something that interests them enough to find out more on another page. If this is the case, you need to make sure you target your list with the right content and information. You also need to continue to build rapport and credibility with your subscribers in order to get them to trust you more.

Something you can also do within the email itself to improve your click through rate is to have more than one link. Perhaps you want to send subscribers to a post on your blog; have a link in your intro, and also have a link at the end of your email as well. Have multiple links that all send subscribers to that one page. The more links you have, the more chances subscribers have of clicking on a link. So don't be afraid to put another link or two in your email, as long as it fits within the context of your email. Don't just put links for the sake of it though. Tie it in with the content or the message you want to convey in your email.

Unsubscribe Rate

The unsubscribe rate is the percentage of people who unsubscribe from your list after receiving emails from you.

Most newer marketers get far too caught up with this – they freak out when people unsubscribe. They don't want to do anything to offend people, and when people unsubscribe they take it personally.

Here's the truth; people will unsubscribe from your list.

They will unsubscribe from your list when you send them a valuable content email, they will unsubscribe when you send them free gifts, they will unsubscribe when you ask for feedback, and yes, they will even unsubscribe when you send them promotional emails.

Having a small percentage of people unsubscribe on each email you send them is normal. Sometimes they just aren't interested in that particular niche anymore, sometimes they have found a different solution to their problem, or sometimes they just don't want to receive your emails anymore.

Don't get caught up with it. You should be consistently sending traffic to your pages to build your list every day, and you should be doing everything you can to bring in more subscribers every day than the number of people who unsubscribe from your list.

Now if your unsubscribe rate is really high, for example higher than 20%, then you need to look closer at the emails you sent them and see why so many people would be unsubscribing from your list.

You always need to track your results, and make adjustments to better improve your email campaigns.

CHAPTER 17

THE BIGGEST EMAIL MARKETING MYTH

The biggest myth about email marketing is that you can create one product, setup one email campaign and just ride that out to riches for the rest of your life.

It's a nice thought; just create a product once, write a few emails, set them up on your autoresponder, then sit back and watch your bank account grow.

Unfortunately, in the real world, it doesn't work like that.

Regardless of how great your product is, how effective your emails are, and how many people you have on your list, things will change over time. Demand for your product will change, other marketers will create products that compete against yours, consumer needs change, and people's interests change as well.

It'd be great if you could do the work once and then make 'automated profits' for the rest of your life. But that doesn't happen. Things will change, and in order to continue to make a living with email marketing, you need to adapt to the changing world, and to the changing needs of your market.

You can't just rely on one product or one email campaign to succeed online. You need to continue to promote multiple products with multiple lists targeting multiple niches.

Always ask yourself, "What else can I offer my subscribers? What do they need now? What are my competitors doing that I'm currently not doing?"

If you don't adapt with your market, you're going to be left behind and you'll soon find that your product and email campaigns will become outdated.

Something else you'll need to adapt to are your traffic sources. Some traffic sources will get saturated with marketers all selling the same thing, other traffic sources simply die out. So you need to establish multiple traffic sources if you want to consistently build your list over time.

Don't just rely on one traffic source. If you do that you're putting your entire online business at risk.

An example of people who do this are those who rely completely on SEO to bring traffic to their site. They optimize their sites and do everything they can to please Google's search engine algorithm. They might see some good traffic for a while, but as soon as Google changes their algorithm, the traffic they were getting completely dries up and they're left with nothing. No rankings, and no traffic. They're back at square one because they made the mistake of relying completely on one source of traffic.

So you need to always pay attention to what's happening in your market. You need to be willing to adapt and change if you want to succeed with your online business in the long term.

CHAPTER 18

HOW TO MAKE MONEY FROM YOUR TRIBE IN THE LONG RUN

So now you know the importance of having to adapt and change to your market and your subscribers' needs, instead of just relying on one product or one email campaign, here's how you can set your online business up for success.

There are really two ways to continue to make money from your subscribers over the long run:

1. Create more products to sell to your list
2. Find more affiliate products to promote to your list

So either way you need to sell more products to your list – the only difference is if you want to create your own products to sell, or focus on promoting affiliate products instead.

There are benefits to both options, but overall it is usually much more profitable to create your own products, especially when you are going to be spending most of your time selling to your subscribers.

Now let's say you're going to create your own products, another major consideration you need to make with your products is the price range.

One option you can take is to create new products that are about the same price range and quality as other products your list has already purchased.

The other option is to create products that are larger, more substantial, and therefore more expensive than the products your subscribers are already purchasing.

The idea with creating more products at a higher price range is that you are able to target your subscribers who are able and willing to pay a higher price for high level course. Obviously there will be a lower percentage of your list who will be able or willing to pay more, but those who are will usually become your most loyal customers.

This gives you the opportunity to continue to provide them with even more solutions and better course, which means you are also able to sell more higher priced course to them.

So how do you go about doing this?

The simple answer is you need to have a sales funnel.

A sales funnel is a collection of products within the same niche that you present to your subscribers over time. The longer they remain on your list, the further they progress through your sales funnel and the more products you will present to them.

Usually a profitable sales funnel begins with building a list of free subscribers when you offer a free gift to visitors in exchange for their email. Once they're on your email list, you build a relationship with them and offer them a low priced product first that is designed to give your customers a 'trial' of what you have to offer and the level of value you provide in your products.

Once your subscriber has bought a product from you and entered your sales funnel, he will be presented with even more higher level products at a higher price tag over time.

A typical sales funnel might look something like this:

- A free offer where you build your list of free subscribers
- A $7-$27 product, which is the frontend product that introduces buyers to your paid products
- A $47-$77 product, which can be a 100 page ebook
- A $97-$297 product, which can be advanced video course
- A $497-$1000 product, which might be a coaching or mentoring program

Obviously the type of products can be altered, and the price points changed as well, but this basic sales funnel should give you an idea of the different types of products you can create and the different price points you should be targeting.

So let's take a look at how this type of sales funnel might work. Let's say you get 5000 free subscribers who signup to your email list. You send them a few content and free gift emails to start off with, then you present them with a low priced entry-level product at $7. Now maybe 10% of your subscribers might buy that product.

Now you have 50 customers, who used to be free subscribers. Those 50 customers are then immediately moved to your buyers list, where you will only promote products of a similar or higher value and price point as the one they already purchased. You then present them with the next product in the sales funnel, which is a more extensive product at a higher price point, and over time you continue to promote the other higher level and more expensive products to your buyers.

The key is to continue to move people through your sales funnel; from free subscribers to buyers of low-priced products, then to buyers of higher-priced products, and then buyers of even higher-priced products.

Obviously the value you provide has to justify the price point for each product, so instead of providing just an eBook, maybe you could create a membership site, or a coaching program. Whatever it is make sure it is far more extensive and far more valuable than other products at a lower price range.

You should of course also continue to provide a lot of high quality content for free as well. The difference now is with your buyers, the free content needs to be even better than it is for your free subscribers.

So you need to always be giving more content, as well as giving better content.

CHAPTER 19

WRAPPING THINGS UP

Successful email marketing isn't something you can just learn once and master.

You need to test things out, track what works, then tweak your campaign to improve your results.

You have to think of email marketing, and your overall online business, with the big picture in mind. You can't just create one product and one email campaign and expect that to make you rich.

You need to build out a proper sales funnel, create multiple email campaigns for each of your products, and track the effectiveness of those campaigns.

You need to stay up to date with what's happening in your niche, what your subscribers are doing, and what they need. If you rest on your laurels after creating just one campaign, you're going to be left behind by your competition.

Most importantly, you need to focus on building a solid relationship with your list. It's about building a relationship with your subscribers, building credibility and rapport, so they will come to know, like and trust you enough to buy from you not just once, but many times over the long run.

Don't think about email marketing with the short term in mind. That's a mistake most people make. They only think about the first sale. They only think about making sales on one product. What they don't realize is that one product isn't enough. You need to have multiple products at multiple price points in your sales funnel if you really want to succeed and make money from your subscribers over the long run.

The connecting of products and programs into a cohesive automation plan is what I help my clients with every day. I coach them through the process to map out their entire client experience and help them create a plan for moving a prospect through the process of warming up to the brand and turning into a lead to become a high-paying client. We also lay out all the technical bits to make that happen and create a punch list of all the content that will need to be created to allow this "connection machine" to share their love (and message) with the world. I find architecting these types of funnels and campaigns FUN. (Yes, really!)

Ok… that's it!

I hope you have enjoyed this email marketing book, and that you go out and actually implement what you have learned. Don't just go through this book and then do nothing with it. That's what a lot of people will do when they buy any type of book, and that's also why most people struggle with their online businesses.

Put this book to use for your email campaigns and build a long term online business that you can be proud of.

You CAN totally do this, but if you feel you need help with anything here in this book, please reach out to me.

You can connect with me online and via social media.

Website: SpellbindingBusinessSchool.com

Facebook: LevitzMarketing

Twitter: JenLevitz

Email: Jen@SpellbindingBusinessSchool.com

I'd be honored to help you with your business. I'm here for you.

Cheers!

Jen Levitz

SpellbindingBusinessSchool.com

ABOUT THE AUTHOR

Jen Levitz is a Business Wizard, Coach, & Strategic Automation & Marketing Consultant as well as the founder of Spellbinding Business School. SpellbindingBusinessSchool.com is dedicated to empowering rapidly growing businesses to serve more people, make more money, work less hours, and have more fun.

At her core, Jen is a techie geek who loves to automate stuff. She believes in fueling small business momentum with client experience centered marketing and automation. Additionally, she brings best practices from 7-figure coaches and information marketers to help her clients share their heart-based messages with prospect and clients more deeply, more consistently, and with less effort.

Jen transforms the lives of mission-driven entrepreneurs around the globe with her expertise. Through her workshops, courses, speeches, and coaching programs, Jen helps her clients to effectively use technology to build strong client relationships and rapidly grow their businesses. She integrates and optimizes technology systems so that rapidly growing businesses can launch successful marketing endeavors throughout the globe.

Jen lives with her husband, son, and 2 cats in Southern California, USA. She loves playing board games, reading books, walking on the beach, being a cheerleader for her clients, and generally geeky out over nerdy things.

Before You Go...

In writing this book, it was my hope and intention to give you a book that would leave you thinking differently about your email marketing, especially when it comes to writing campaigns.

If it shifted anything for you, would you do me a favor and share it with others?

There are so many people that think that writing emails are hard and complicated. But it really is as simple as what I shared with you in this book. So please share the wealth, ok?

You've got this!

Thank You